# WALKS

# HERTS & E

# VOL 4

Founded: 1957

Registered Charity No: 1068733

 **Bishop's Stortford & District Footpaths Association**

Safeguarding your Public Rights of Way in and around Bishop's Stortford

PUBLISHED BY

BISHOP'S STORTFORD & DISTRICT
FOOTPATHS ASSOCIATION

REGISTERED
CHARITY NO.
1068733

# Bishop's Stortford & District Footpaths Association
## Registered Charity No. 1068733

The Association was founded in 1957 to "preserve, protect and maintain Public Rights of Way in the Herts and Essex border area around Bishop's Stortford".

Membership is open to anyone who wishes to assist in protecting rights of way. Members receive our twice yearly newsletter with news and discussion of rights of way problems and activities and programmes of guided walks – opportunities to discover less well known paths, meet like-minded people, make new friends and discover new horizons.

The Association also maintains a website with news and information, including a gallery of photographs.

Even if you do not walk much, your support as a member would be useful. The more members we represent the more influence we can exert on various authorities who should protect rights of way.

---

<u>Membership Application</u>
Please refer to the Association website for details of membership.
www.walksaroundstortford.org.uk

# THE BOOKLET

This is the eighth book of Walks in Herts and Essex published by Bishop's Stortford and District Footpaths Association. The Association's aim is to safeguard public rights of way within a 10 mile radius of Bishop's Stortford. We hope you will enjoy the Walks and appreciate the local countryside and that your use of the paths will help to keep them open.

The 21 Walks in this booklet use some paths which have been included in Walks in previous booklets, but we have tried to keep the Walks varied and have explored some areas not previously covered.

Our local countryside is undulating, with some scattered woodland and river valleys, with good views from higher ground. There is much historic interest, including the sites of three castles, an abbey, an iron-age fort and numerous churches, some dating back to Saxon and Norman times. Many villages have fine timbered buildings up to 500 years old, including thatched inns. The area has several windmills, the site of an important Roman settlement and two Roman roads.

The surface soil sits on Boulder Clay, underlayed by chalk which is sometimes visible where streams have cut into the landscape. Boulder Clay grows good cereal crops but can be very muddy when wet. Sturdy walking boots are recommended in all but the driest weather.

While great care has been taken to make directions in this booklet as accurate as possible, the Association cannot accept responsibility for errors or omissions or changes in details and landmarks mentioned. Over a period of time, changes take place to field boundaries, fences and hedges and even new housing developments appear. Additionally, the threat of airport expansion is never very far away.

The Walks are intended to require only the text and the sketch maps in the booklet. However, it adds to enjoyment to see what surrounds you and the Ordnance Survey Explorer maps which are scaled to 1:25000 are excellent for walking.
The following Ordnance Survey Explorer maps are useful for the Walks.

| Walks 10,19,21 | Explorer 183 – Chelmsford & The Rodings |
|---|---|
| Walks 1,2,3,5,6,7,8,10,11,13,15,17,20 | Explorer 194 – Hertford & Bishop's Stortford |
| Walks 4,5,9,10,12,14,16,18 | Explorer 195 – Braintree & Saffron Walden |

Walk no 5 – Explorer 194 or 195 may be used
Walk no 10 – Explorer 183,194 & 195.  Walk no 12 – Explorer 183 & 195

If you find problems with any path, such as obstructions by barbed wire, locked gates, broken stiles, broken footbridges, missing sign posts or ploughed fields where the path has not been re-instated, please report them to the Rights of Way Officer at the appropriate County Council Office and inform the Association Paths Secretary. Refer to the footpath problems section at the end of the booklet.

Our thanks are due to all those who helped to produce the booklet and test the Walks.

Joyce Chapman
Paul Elliot
Phil Tripp

2012

# THE INDEX

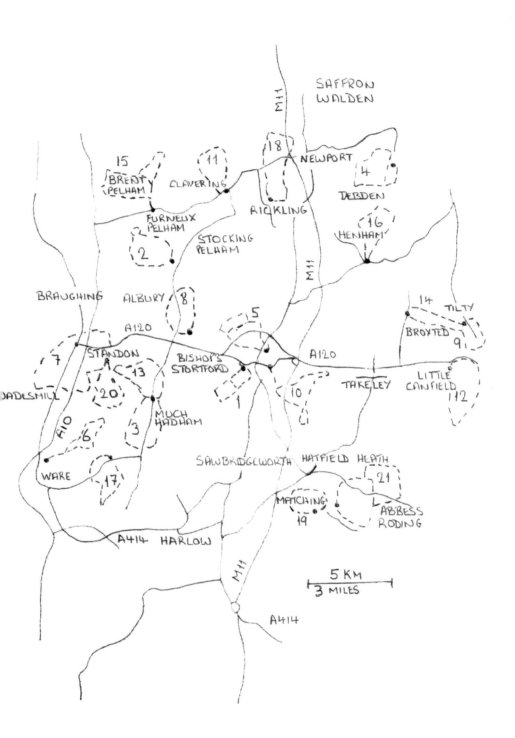

# 1 BISHOP'S STORTFORD (BISHOP'S PARK CENTRE), BURY GREEN, ASH VALLEY, GREEN STREET

**Distance:**

**Main Walk: 10.0 kms/6.25 miles**

**Short Walk: 7.5 kms/4.7 miles**

*The walk may start at Burghley Avenue or Dukes Ride, close to the Tesco store at grid ref TL461216.*

*The walk goes through open countryside and passes through the picturesque village of Bury Green and if the longer walk is taken, overlooks the Ash Valley, where there are some splendid views. On summer weekends, it may be possible to watch Polo matches at Hoecroft Lane.*

Point A – Burghley Avenue / Dukes Ride

Proceed along Dukes Ride for 125 metres. Turn right onto the Hertfordshire Way (FP17) and cross the road.

CAUTION

This is a busy road and needs to be crossed with extreme care as the views in both directions are partially obscured by bushes. Continue ahead, along the Hertfordshire Way, keeping trees on right and field on left. At the corner of the field, go through a gap in the hedgerow. Turn left along a wide grassy area. Shortly after, walk through a gap on the right and bear left, keeping a hedgerow on the left and field on the right.

Shortly after, ignore a footpath crossing and cross a concrete bridge. Carry straight on keeping electricity pylons to the right. Just before a second concrete bridge, turn right onto a waymarked path, keeping a ditch / stream on the left and field on right. Enter a wood, still keeping the stream on the left.

Emerging from the wood, turn left across the stream and then right with the stream now on the right. Continue to the lane.

Turn right onto the lane and continue to the road junction in Bury Green. Bear left. Follow the road for 750 metres, passing Clinton's Farm on the left, leaving the village and later ignoring the first footpath to the left until a second footpath junction is reached on the left, Point B.

Point B – Short Walk

Continue ahead until Hoecroft Lane is reached on the right. Turn right onto the main walk at Hoecroft Lane, Point D.

Point B – Main Walk

Here, take the right-hand footpath which goes at right angles to the road, ignoring the path which goes left, and keeping the hedge on the right and later entering a thicket. Emerge from the thicket, cross a plank bridge and go through the kissing gate into the field with horse paddocks. Continue ahead towards a group of trees, following the waymarked arrows. Before the trees, go through a gate and follow left edge of field with wooden fence on left for about 60 metres to a kissing gate on the left. Go through the kissing gate and cross the track and follow the path through the middle of the thicket.

Emerge from the thicket, cross a plank bridge and follow path with trees and hedge on left. At the corner of a field, cross another plank bridge and turn immediately right with hedge on right. Follow this line, later with Bush Wood on right to a T junction, Point C.

Point C

NOTE: *Here, there is a wooden bench with splendid views overlooking the Ash Valley.* Turn right here. Follow the bridleway ahead for 1 km, mainly with hedgerow on the left until the left corner of a field is reached. Go through a gap in the hedge and pass the cottage on the left to reach a road.

NOTE: *This is Acremore Street between Bury Green and Hadham Ford.* Turn right. Walk uphill to Hoecroft Lane, Point D.

<u>Point D – Hoecroft Lane (Main Walk)</u>
Turn left onto the Public Byway, Hoecroft Lane. Continue along this lane to a road. Turn left. Walk along the road for 200 metres, passing Millfield Cottage on the left and then turn right onto a footpath. Proceed with hedge on right, eventually coming to a plank bridge on the right. Cross the hedge via the plank bridge. Carry on downhill passing a horse paddock on the right to a road.

This is Green Street. Turn right onto the road. Continue to the T junction. Cross the road. Follow the footpath along the field edge with hedge and stream/ditch on the right. At the path junction beyond power lines, turn left. At the end of the hedge on the right, go through a wide gap on the right, following the wide space ahead to a gap in the hedge on the right. Go through the gap and follow the path with hedgerow and trees on the left back to the Start at the Bishop's Park Centre.

CAUTION
Take care when crossing the busy road at the end of the field.

MAP 1

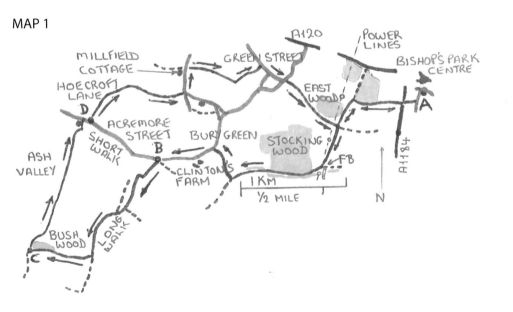

## 2 BARLEYCROFT END / FURNEUX PELHAM AND THE HORMEADS

**Point A: 11.7 kms/7.3 miles**
**Point B: 10.7 kms/6.7 miles**
*This Walk may start from Furneux Pelham Village Hall in Barleycroft End, Point A (grid ref TL435277) or Furneux Pelham Church, Point B (grid ref TL431279). A small loop is added at Point D to make a figure of eight which takes in Great Hormead.*
*Refreshments are available in Barleycroft End (Brewery Tap P.H) and Great Hormead (Three Tuns P.H).*

Point A – Furneux Pelham Village Hall, Barleycroft End

Turn left out of the Hall car park. After the Brewery Tap P.H, turn left. Follow the road to the Church on the right, Point B.

Point B – Furneux Pelham Church

After the church, turn right onto the footpath and go through the kissing gate. Follow the right hand edge of the pasture to the end. Go through a kissing gate and across the footbridge. Go through the thicket, crossing a track junction into a wooded area. Exiting the wooded area, head for a waymarked post. Cross the field to the right corner of a thicket ahead. Turn left. Shortly after, there is a corner of a derelict wall and a path junction. Bear right onto the wide path and a short distance later, take the left fork and go through the gap in the trees. Keep the hedge on the left until Great Hormead Park wood is reached, Point C.

Point C – Great Hormead Park wood

Turn left onto the Permissive Footpath and after 75 metres, leave the footpath and turn right into the wood. NOTE: *If permission is withdrawn, enter the wood directly in front and bear left to join the path.*

Follow the path and exit the wood after 350 metres, staying on the byway for a further 1 kilometre to a cross track junction, Point D.

Point D through Great Hormead and return to Point D

Turn right and at a left hand bend, leave the track and continue ahead, crossing a stile. Follow the path through a pasture down to the road. Turn left onto the road and after the Three Tuns P.H, turn left and go up Horseshoe Hill. Follow the road passing the War Memorial on the left, continuing to St. Nicholas Church on the right. Turn left onto the Hertfordshire Way. Follow the path between two fields to a gap in the hedge to complete the small loop, Point D.

Point D

Turn right. Follow the path down to the road at Little Hormead. Cross the road. Follow the path between farm buildings and follow the right edge of a pasture with hedgerow on right, later with field on right, hedgerow and stream on left. Cross stream on the left and go through a gap in the hedge and turn right, now with a field on the left and hedgerow on the right. After 100 metres, at a track junction, turn left. Cross the field and enter the Mutfords complex, turning left and immediately right, exiting the complex. Follow the driveway to a waymark post at a slight right hand bend. Turn left and follow the path across the field to the right corner of a hedgerow. (This is the definitive route).
NOTE: *Alternative route. Exit the Mutfords complex. After 50 metres, there is a ditch on the left at right-angles to the driveway. Follow the wide grass verge on the right-hand side of the ditch, until the corner of the hedgerow is reached above.* Continue to the end of the long field. Go through

the gap and turn right, keeping hedgerow on right, later crossing a field to a wood. Enter the wood. Take a left fork in the wood and exit the wood, following the definitive path across the field, to a large house at Rotten Row, Point E.

NOTE: *Alternatively, follow the wide grass verge along the edge of the wood to the driveway.*

Point E – Rotten Row

Turn left. Follow the driveway past a Cricket field on the left to the right corner of a wood.

Continue ahead with the wood on the left to the corner. Cross the large field to the fence at the far end and go through a kissing gate and across a pasture, through a thicket and another pasture to a kissing gate. Go through the kissing gate. Pass cottages on the left and emerge at the road. Turn left. At the T junction, turn right and return to the Start at the Village Hall, Point A or the Church, Point B.

MAP 2

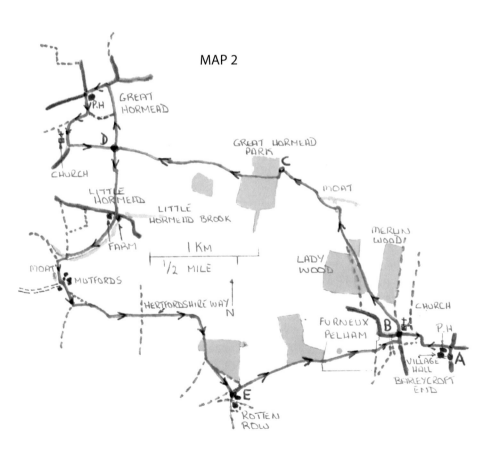

# 3 MUCH HADHAM, WIDFORD PARISH, KETTLE GREEN

## Distance: 9.7 kms/6.1 miles

*Park opposite Ye Olde Red Lion Hotel in Much Hadham where there is ample roadside parking, (grid ref TL 428197). This is a contrasting walk, initially close to the River Ash, with a wide variety of scenery, taking in meadows, woodland and farmland and crossing the route of the old disused Buntingford railway line twice.*

Point A – Ye Olde Red Lion, Much Hadham

With Ye Olde Red Lion Hotel on the right, walk a short distance and turn left and go down Church Lane. Follow the road round to the right, passing the church entrance on the left. At a house named 'Two Bridges', leave the road and go through a kissing gate and keep left, ignoring the footpath to the right. Continue over the well made footbridge over the River Ash, then over the pasture and later crossing a driveway via two kissing gates. Continue over meadows until you reach a road. Turn left and follow the road round, sharp right, then sharp left. After 30 metres, turn right into Sidehill Wood, following the bridleway with the wood on the left and the meadow on the right, later crossing to the left side of a fence. Continue along the bridleway to the road. Join the road with Bourne Lodge on the right. Continue along the road to a T junction, Point B, Widford Road.

Point B – Widford Road

Cross the road and bear left onto a bridleway, shortly after following a right field edge, later passing a Water Works on the left. Continue onto a concrete driveway to a lane. Cross the lane and continue for 250 metres to a footpath crossing.

NOTE: *Widford Church can be seen at the top of the hill in the distance.*

Take the path to the right through a kissing gate and after 50 metres on the right, cross a footbridge over the River Ash, emerging into a meadow. Follow the left edge of the meadow, ignoring a stile on the left and go through an opening into the next field.

NOTE: *This is the crossing point of the former Buntingford railway line.*

Bear left and go up the wide grassy track a short distance and follow the right field edge with the trees on the right. After 50 metres, leave the treeline and go diagonally left up the hill into a thicket at the top of the hill. Continue through the thicket and join a lane, Upper Crackney Lane. Continue along the lane, passing Little Blakesware Farm on the left and shortly after, meeting a bridleway crossing. Continue ahead to a wood, Blakes Bushes. Follow the right outside edge of the wood for about 500 metres. At a sharp corner of the wood, continue ahead, leaving the wood behind. Kettle Green can be seen in the distance. Proceed along this bridleway to Moat Farm.

NOTE: *Observe the picturesque moat, where there may be an abundance of birdlife.*

Follow the bridleway round to the left, leaving Moat Farm behind to meet a road, Point C.

Point C – Moat Farm Entrance/Exit

Join the road at the bend, bearing right and passing the entrance to Old Hall Farm on the left. Continue over the humpback bridge.

NOTE: *The bridge crosses over the old trackbed of the disused Buntingford railway line.*

Shortly after the bridge, turn sharp left onto Brand's Lane.

NOTE: *This is a Restricted Byway and is not open to motorised traffic other than farm traffic.*
Continue on the lane for about 1 km, passing farms on the left, to a T Junction, Cox Lane.
Turn sharp right onto Cox Lane, which is initially a narrow lane with tall hedges on the left and right and later becomes a wider track.
As the wider track later sweeps round to the left, continue ahead on the much narrower lane, descending into Much Hadham. At the junction with the High Street, turn left and return to the Start at Point A.

MAP 3

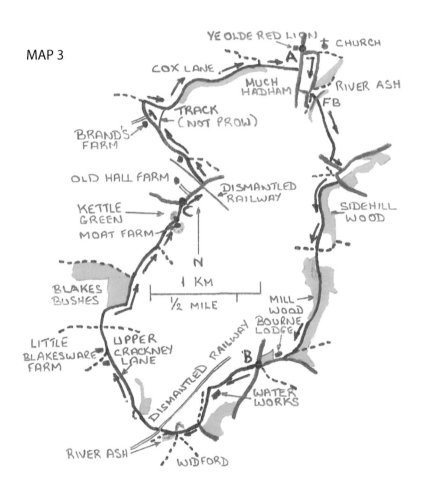

# 4  DEBDEN

**Option A: Distance: 7.5 kms/4.7 miles**
**Option B: Distance: 6.5 kms/4.1 miles**
*This is a Walk around the Debden area, starting from Debden Church (grid ref TL 551332). There are two options from Point C of this Walk. Option A and Option B consist of well made paths.*

Point A – Debden Church

Walk along the path with the Church on the left and at a T Junction and bridge with a lake ahead, turn right and follow the path uphill to a road. Cross the road with care and continue straight ahead to the corner of a wood. Here, bear left and follow track downhill with electricity poles alongside. Approaching the house in front, turn left along the diverted footpath then turn right with pond on right, then turn left down the drive almost to the road, where there is another driveway on the right, Point B.

Point B – Entrance to Brick House Farm and Midsummer House

Take the left of two paths and immediately cross a stile at an electronically operated gate and pass Midsummer House on the left and cross another stile. Immediately after, cross a third stile on the left and walk across a pasture towards the far right corner. Cross another stile and walk across the right edge of the pasture to a split in the paths. Here, take the narrow right path with hedgerows on both sides and the stream, Debden Water on the left, later across a meadow, still keeping the stream on your left. Keep straight ahead to the corner of a wood. Follow the left edge of the wood for 100 metres and then turn left across a well made footbridge. Cross the field straight ahead to another wood in front. Walk up the path through the wood to a road. Turn left and follow the road for 225 metres to Ringers Barn on the right. Enter Ringers Barn and go to the left of a metal gate and follow the path, sharply to the left, passing the barn on the right and then follow a good farm track. Pass a trig point and then at a byway, bear left and continue ahead to a road. Turn left along the road for 100 metres and at the left bend, leave the road and continue ahead past Waldegraves Farm on the left along a byway to a Path Junction with a wood on the left, Point C.

Point C

Here there are two options, Option A and Option B.

Option A – Point C

Continue ahead alongside the right edge of Cabbage Wood. At the far corner of the wood, follow a kink in the track downhill to a lane with a thatched cottage on the right. Turn left onto the lane and after Rook End Cottage on left, bear left diagonally across the field to a well made footbridge. After the footbridge, turn left and continue for 750 metres to a gap at the corner of a field. Go through the gap and go straight ahead past the corner of a hedge with a brick wall behind it. Continue to the driveway, turn right, then turn left and back to the Start at the church, Point A.

Option B – Point C

Bear left and enter the wood via a kissing gate. Walk along the track through the wood. Emerging from the wood, follow the path downhill with fields on both sides to a bridge over the stream. After the bridge, turn right and follow the path back to the church, Point A.

MAP 4

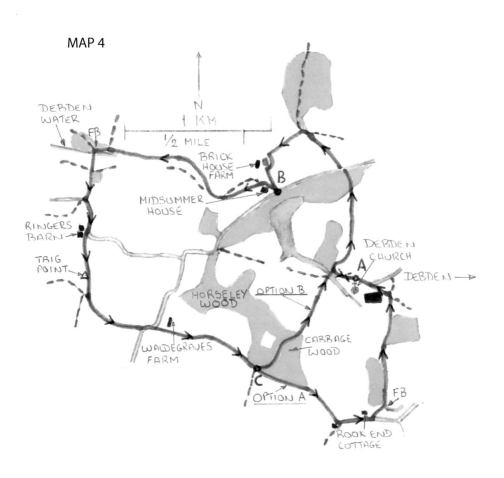

## 5 BISHOP'S STORTFORD, HOGGATE'S WOOD RYE STREET

**Distance:**
**Main Walk: 6.2 kms/3.9 miles**
**Short Walk: 5.0 kms/3.1 miles**

*A four (or three) mile walk in unspoilt country on the north west side of Bishop's Stortford. Start at Grange Paddocks (grid ref TL488221) where there is a car park.*

Point A – Grange Paddocks, Rye Street
From the car park, return to Rye Street (Point A) and cross the road and walk up Lindsey Road almost opposite. At the top, cross a road and go through the gap opposite. Follow down the right hand side of the playing fields and at the bottom right hand corner go ahead across the track through some trees and enter a large scrubby pasture. Take the middle one of the three paths, leading diagonally across the pasture and then up the hill to a gate and stile at the top. Opposite the stile, a footpath leads down, curves right then follows all the way up the edge of Hoggate's Wood. At the top, turn left to go under the by-pass then right over a high stile on to a faint path leading diagonally across the field to a stile in the far left corner, where a notice gives warning of galloping horses. Continue along the right hand side of the next small field and cross the gallop track to join a gravel road, Point B.

NOTE: *For a shorter walk turn right here and go down the track to Point C and rejoin the main route, where it becomes concrete.*

Point B
For the main walk, turn left and walk up the track as far as a tall radio mast. Here, turn right and passing a house on your left, continue along an earth track for 700 metres, always with a hedge on your left.

At Walnuttree Cottages, turn right onto a grass path, again with a hedge on the left, leading down to rejoin the farm track, Point C.

Point C
Go left to the bottom of the track, then before the barrier, take a signed path to the right leading under the bypass. Immediately after the bridge, turn right and follow a path parallel to the road. At the top, turn left and continue along a path with a hedge on your left. At the corner of the field, go through the gap and continue straight on, down and up across two arable fields. Emerging on a lane, go left down a rough track to meet a stony road. Turn left again and at a blue converted barn on a corner, turn right and go down to Rye Street, Point D.

Point D
Cross the busy road with care.
NOTE: *For a short cut back to Point A, turn right and continue for 330 metres.* For the main walk turn left and then after 250 metres, just after the last house (no 102), turn right down a lane leading to the railway. Just before the crossing, go right through a kissing gate onto a path leading to a footbridge. Follow the left hand bank of the River Stort back to the car park at Grange Paddocks.

MAP 5

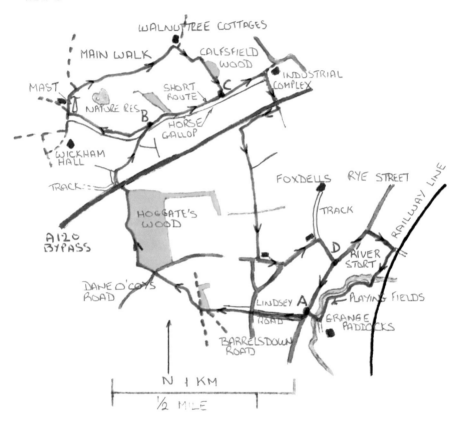

# 6 WARE (WODSON PARK SPORTS AND LEISURE CENTRE), BARWICK FORD

**Distance: 11.2 kms/7.0 miles**

*This Walk starts and finishes at Wodson Park Sports and Leisure Centre, Ware (grid ref TL355157). Please use their facilities. There is a cafeteria inside. This walk is an anti-clockwise circular walk. It mainly consists of bridlepaths with a few footpaths. Barwick Ford, a point of interest, is approximately the half way point.*

Point A – Wodson Park Sports and Leisure Centre

Exit the Sports Centre Car Park and turn right and walk 100 metres to the Moles Farm Entrance Gates. Follow the bridlepath to the Farm and walk between the farm buildings and continue for 800 metres where the surface changes to a road with houses on the right. At a road T Junction, turn right and follow the road for 200 metres until there is a bridlepath on the right and left. Take the left path and follow downhill for 300 metres to a T Junction, Point B.

Point B

Turn right onto the Hertfordshire Way and proceed ahead, later crossing a driveway and then following the course of the River Rib on the left. Later, at a finger post, turn right and go uphill through a tunnel of trees. At the top, at a road is Hollytrees. Turn right and go downhill for 100metres to a right bend and turn left through white gates.

Pass Timber Hall on the left, then fence on left, scrub on right. Before the end of the scrub, the Hertfordshire Way curves to the right. Ignore the path to the right and carry straight on and cross a field heading for the left corner of the wood. Proceed along left edge of wood to a cross path junction. Go straight across, passing a lone tree on the right. Sawtrees Farm and Sawtrees Wood can be seen in the distance. Turn right at a far corner of a thicket, then shortly after, turn left across a field to a road. Cross the road and enter Sawtrees Farm bearing right, then exiting the farm. Here, bear left and head diagonally across the field to Sawtrees Wood. Enter the wood and follow the track to the bottom, where the track bears slightly left. Here, turn right for a short distance to a road with a house on the left. Turn left onto the road and cross Barwick Ford via a footbridge to the entrance to Great Barwick Manor on the left, Point C.

Point C – Great Barwick Manor (Harcamlow Way)

Enter Great Barwick Manor and turn immediately left and follow Harcamlow Way to a forked track junction at the corner of a field. Turn right.

NOTE: *This is a convenient resting place. There are two naturally made benches here.*

Follow the path uphill with a hedge on the right, field on the left. At the next field, follow the same line ahead. At the top of the hill, continue with a wood on the left, a field and an airstrip on the right. At the far corner of the wood, follow the bridlepath to the left and continue along this path to a farm entrance and T Junction.

Turn left towards a wood on the right. Note the tumuli near the near corner of the wood. Keep to the right, ignoring the track which bends to the left and follow the path downhill with the wood on the right.

Go through a gate and enter a meadow and shortly after turn right.

Cross the split River Rib via two well made footbridges. After the last bridge, bear left across the meadow towards a path junction and the disued church (Thundridge Old Church) on the right. Go through a kissing gate to the track which passes in front.

Turn left onto the Hertfordshire Way and follow for 200 metres to the bridlepath on the right.

This is Point B on the outgoing walk. Turn right and follow the path uphill to the road.

CAUTION
Take care at this junction, as this is a blind corner. Keep children and dogs under control. Also take care when walking on the road towards the next road junction or the left.

At the road, turn right and after 200 metres, turn left onto a road which is signed as a cul-de-sac. Continue as the road changes to a bridleway. Retrace your steps through Moles Farm to the Start at Wodson Park Sports and Leisure Centre, Point A.

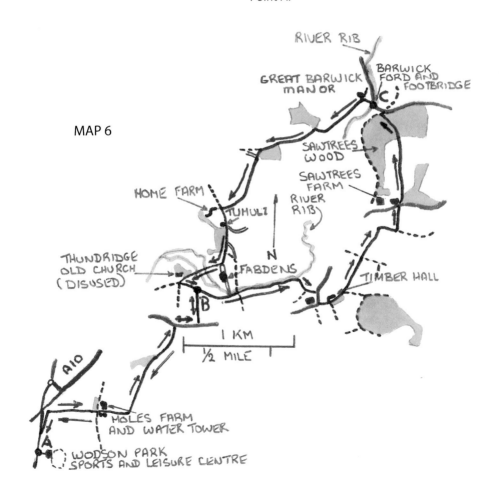

MAP 6

# 7 STANDON, COLLIERS END, POTTER'S GREEN, LEVENS GREEN

**Distance: 13.2 kms/8.2 miles**

*This Walk starts from the front of St. Mary's Church in Standon (grid ref TL396222). Park on the wide High Street near the church. This walk takes in open countryside, woodland and meadows with splendid views of Standon and later the north Hertfordshire countryside.*

## Point A – St. Mary's Church, Standon

With the church on the left, walk a short distance along the High Street and turn right into Paper Mill Lane. NOTE: *Observe the Standon Puddingstone at the junction placed there in 1904 and the oak tree next to it planted in 1911 to commemorate the coronation of King George V.*

Walk along Paper Mill Lane, ignoring the first footpath to the left before the ford. Cross the footbridge next to the ford and after the ford turn left onto the footpath, Point B.

## Point B – footpath after the ford

Go along the meadow, with the river on the left.

NOTE: *At the highest point look back towards Standon and observe the landscape.*

At the end of the meadow, go through kissing gate and with Standon Lordship on the left, turn right and walk along a lane to a road.

Cross the road and follow a track uphill with hedgerow on right, continuing to a finger post. Here, turn left and cross a field to Plashes Wood and then turn left at the wood, then right at the corner.

Follow the edge of the wood until a lane in front is reached. Here, turn right and enter the wood. Shortly after, bear left and head towards Plashes Farm. At the farm, turn left onto a driveway, then immediately right at the corner of the farm, re-enter the wood and descend through the wood towards the A10 dual carriageway.

At the bottom, go under the A10 and follow a field edge, initially with ditch on right. Continue following the field edge and head to St. Mary's Church at Colliers End, emerging on the right hand side of the church at the road, Point C.

## Point C – St. Mary's Church, Colliers End

Cross the road. Turn left then right, going up Labdens Lane to a right hand bend. Continue straight ahead along the right side of a field into the next field.

Turn left and follow the left edge of the field towards a wood, then follow the right edge of the wood into the dip, where there is a stream/ditch.

Turn right and follow the perimeter of the field, initially with stream/ditch on right, later with a small wood on the right until a well made footbridge is reached on the right. Cross the footbridge. Potter's Green comes into view.

Follow the field paths to Potter's Green. Cross a stile and head towards the back gate of a property. Go through the gate and onto the driveway (The Gables) to the left bend in the driveway. Here, turn right onto a track, Point D.

## Point D – Potter's Green

Follow the track and go between horse paddocks and later a cross-field path to the left edge of a hedgerow. Go through a kissing gate and follow the same line with hedge on left and cross a stile.

Walk across a pasture to another stile. Cross the stile, the footbridge across a stream and a gate. Follow the right field edge and at the end, go through a gate and turn right onto a track and at the entrance to High Trees Farm, turn right onto a lane and at the house named the Paddocks on the right, bear left, leaving the lane and following the byway to Levens Green, Point E.

Point E – Levens Green

Cross the road. Follow the byway through a wood and on reaching a road, turn right. Follow the road for 150 metres, then turn left and cross the field to the right corner of a hedgerow.

Cross the plank footbridge and follow the left edge of a field downhill to Hole Farm. Go through the farm and exiting the farm, follow the left of two paths and descend down the pasture to the A10.

CAUTION: Cross the A10 with care and follow the path to the road. (This is the road into Puckeridge). Turn right and cross the A120 with care.

Proceed along the concrete path until there is a footpath on the left, just before the A10 bridge crosses in front.

Follow the footpath on the left and ascend to the top.

NOTE: *This footpath is exposed to the elements. Observe the fine view of Standon ahead.*

Continue along the footpath, later crossing a road and then joining a lane from the right.

Descend to the ford and return to St. Mary's Church at Standon, Point A.

## MAP 7

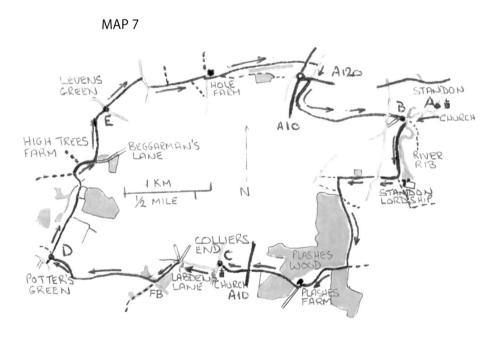

## 8    LITTLE HADHAM, ALBURY, PATMORE HEATH, UPWICK GREEN, HADHAM HALL

**Distance: 7.7 kms/4.8 miles**

*This Walk starts at St.Cecilia's Church, grid ref TL446227. There is a large car park behind the church. The Walk crosses mainly farmland. At Patmore Heath, there is a nature reserve, which is a Site of Special Scientific Interest (SSSI) and has an information board.*

Point A – St. Cecilia's Church

With the church porch on your right, follow the path ahead between the fields. Cross a footbridge over the River Ash and head to Albury Road. Opposite is a track by a public footpath sign. Follow the track with hedge and field on the right. At a bungalow on the left, bear right onto the footpath as the track goes ahead.

Cross a footbridge, turn right and after 75 metres, turn right again to follow the waymarked path to Albury, keeping the stream/ditch on your right.

Cross a second footbridge and continue on the edge of the field path to reach a farm track which crosses in front. Turn right onto the track and after a few metres, turn immediately left, crossing a footbridge. Continue along the stream which is now on your left, walking along the edge of a plantation. Continue beside the stream for 200 metres to a second plantation.

Bear right following the path through the trees. Emerge from the plantation onto a track. Turn right for only a few metres until you reach the T Junction at the top.

Turn left and continue to the road near Albury Church, Point B.

Point B

Cross the road and enter the field through the kissing gate. Turn half right across the field.

NOTE: *Here, there is a tree planted in commemoration of the Coronation of King George VI.*

Head downhill, passing to the left of a large clump of trees around a pond. Continue to the bottom of the field. Follow the field edge with the River Ash on the right, heading to a footbridge which crosses the River Ash.

At the footbridge, cross the River Ash and continue up a track to the road. Turn left for 45 metres, then turn right along a narrow alley by the side of a pillar box. On reaching Patmore Heath, turn right onto the road for 250 metres and then right by a fingerpost onto a lane, leaving Patmore Heath behind.

NOTE: *Patmore Heath Nature Reserve is an ideal place to explore.*

Continue along the lane for 625 metres to reach a road.

Turn right and immediately left to follow a farm track. The track continues all the way to Upwick Green, joining a metalled lane by a pond on the right.

Follow the lane ahead and at the road junction, turn left.

Walk along the road for 300 metres to Upwick Hall Drive on your right, Point C.

Point C – Upwick Hall Drive

Turn right into Upwick Hall Drive. As the Drive turns right into houses, continue ahead on the grassy track, later with a hedge on the left. At a track junction, curve right, following the track to Hadham Hall.

Enter the grounds of Hadham Hall through a gap and immediately turn right, passing between two ponds. Follow the path round through an archway.

At a pillar box on the left, turn right with a pond on the right and follow the tree-lined path to a lane. The church at the start comes into view, slightly to the left.

Turn left onto the lane and return to the church, Point A.

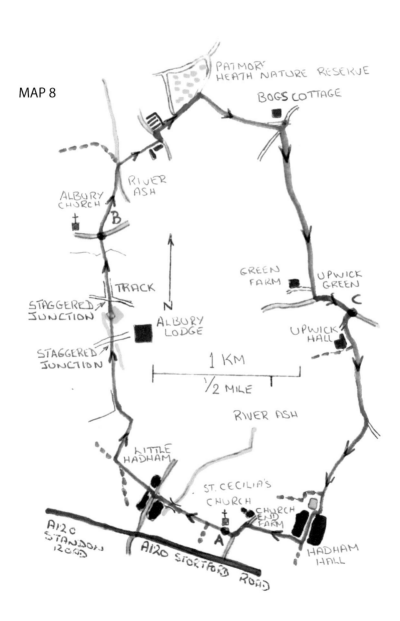

MAP 8

PATMOR HEATH NATURE RESERVE

BOGS COTTAGE

RIVER ASH

ALBURY CHURCH

B

STAGGERED JUNCTION

TRACK

N

GREEN FARM

UPWICK GREEN

C

STAGGERED JUNCTION

ALBURY LODGE

UPWICK HALL

1 KM

½ MILE

RIVER ASH

LITTLE HADHAM

ST. CECILIA'S CHURCH

CHURCH END FARM

A12 c STANDON ROAD

A120 STORTFORD ROAD

A

HADHAM HALL

# 9 TILTY, DUTON HILL, GREAT EASTON, LITTLE EASTON

**Distance: 10.5 kms/6.6 miles**

*This Walk starts at Tilty Church (St. Mary the Virgin) car park (grid ref TL600265) and passes through Duton Hill, Great Easton and Little Easton and passes by the Gardens of Easton Lodge.*

Point A –Tilty Church

Go through the car park kissing gate. Head down the pasture to the bottom, where there is a disused watermill from the 18th century.

NOTE: *On the right of the pasture, there are remains of the 12th century Cistercian Abbey.*

Go through the gate at the bottom of the pasture. Turn right onto the lane, later turning right at a brook, keeping the line of trees and the brook on the left to meet a road. At the road, turn left and after 25 metres, turn right and follow the road uphill to Duton Hill, passing the Three Horseshoes P.H on the right. Exiting the village, opposite Duton Hill Farm, turn right onto a footpath. Head downhill to the bottom. Cross a staggered junction via a plank bridge with railings. Head uphill to a cross path junction at a hedge. Turn right with the hedge on the left and head towards Great Easton, passing the Village Hall on the right, Point B.

Point B – Great Easton

Follow the road downhill, passing the Swan P.H on the right. At the bottom of the hill, there is a footbridge crossing the brook.

NOTE: *This is the River Chelmer.*

Before the footbridge, turn left onto a footpath, with the brook on the right. After approx. 200 metres, emerge into a field. Follow the right edge of the field with the brook on the right for a further 800 metres,

also passing to the left of a thicket and reaching a footbridge on the right. Cross the footbridge and turn left.

NOTE: *This is Fleck Bridge.*

Continue along the path, later crossing a field. Cross a footbridge and turn left, passing a water station on the right and later meeting the road, Duck Street, Point C.

Point C – Duck Street, Little Easton

Turn right onto the road heading to Little Easton. Shortly after the 30mph sign, there are two houses on the left, Hillbrook Cottage and White Gables and the start of two footpaths. Take the second footpath at White Gables with wooden fencing on each side, later with large lawns on the right and scrub on the left. At the far end of the lawns, go through a kissing gate. Turn left, crossing an earth bridge which separates two ponds. At the forked junction of two grassy paths, take the left path uphill. Take the path through the church graveyard to reach a stile and road, Point D.

Point D – Little Easton Church

Turn right, passing the church on the right. Walk along the road passing the pond on the left and later the Gardens of Easton Lodge on the right to Brook End Farm. Here, turn right onto the farm track. Before the stables, bear right onto a path between horse paddocks on the left and right, heading towards a clump of trees ahead. At the clump of trees, turn left and immediately right with a field and wire fence on the left and an overgrown thicket on the right. At the end of the field, turn right onto a green lane. Immediately, a road with a sharp bend is reached. Bear right. Continue on this road for 750 metres to Cherith House on the left, Point E.

NOTE: *This is also known as the Harcamlow Way. This is a long distance footpath between Harlow and Cambridge and follows the route back to Tilty Church.*

Point E – Cherith House
Immediately before Cherith House, turn left onto the footpath following the field edge to the bottom.
At the bottom right corner of the field, cross a footbridge over a stream and through a gate into a horse paddock. Follow the left edge of the paddock.

Slightly to the right of the top left corner of the paddock, go through a large gate and straight ahead to cross a stile to join the road.
Cross the road. Follow the footpath uphill to a ditch in front. Here, turn right and after approx. 300 metres, turn left. Follow this path to the road.
NOTE: *This is an exposed part of the Walk with no shelter.*
At the road, turn right. After approx 300 metres, turn left and return to Tilty Church car park at the start, Point A.

MAP 9

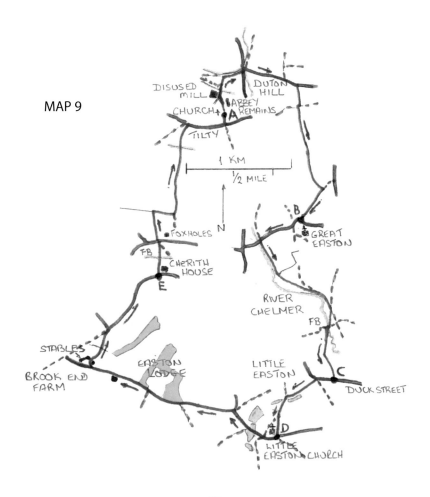

# 10 BISHOP'S STORTFORD, RUSHY MEAD NATURE RESERVE, GREAT HALLINGBURY

**Distance:**

**Long Walk: 12.2 kms/7.6 miles**

**Main Walk: 10.5 kms/6.5 miles**

*This Walk starts at the Link Road Car Park in the centre of Bishop's Stortford (grid ref TL489215). Points of interest include the Castle Mound, War Memorial, Rushy Mead Nature Reserve, St. Giles Church and the Tudor style cottages in Great Hallingbury.*

Point A – Link Road Car Park

Walk round Castle Mound clockwise and walk in between the Markwell Pavilion on the right and the War Memorial on the left, reaching the road. Turn left and then cross the road and continue along the riverbank with river on the right. Cross the second road and continue on river bank with the river on the left. Take a footpath at Southmill Lock no. 1 over the river and walk along the river, with the river now on the right. Ignore the first footpath on the left. Continue along the towpath until reaching Rushy Mead Nature Reserve and take the next path to the left, up through the Nature Reserve onto Hallingbury Road. Straight across is Jenkins Lane. Cross road with care.

CAUTION

This is a fast busy road, with impaired visibility to the left and right.

Walk up Jenkins Lane to a very sharp left turn at the top. Here, take the footpath downhill with hedge on right and horse schooling arena on left to a stone bridge over a stream. Go through a few trees and diagonally left, cross a field and through the motorway underpass. Turn left at a field and shortly after, enter a second field through a gap and turn right, keeping a hedge on the right and the field on the left.

St. Giles Church, Great Hallingbury is straight ahead. At the end of the field, cross a stile and almost immediately go through a gate on the left into the Church graveyard. Pass to the right of the church to meet the road, Point B.

Point B – St. Giles Church, Great Hallingbury

NOTE: *At this point, it is possible to add 1.5 kms if wished, by turning right along the road by the Church.*

Point B - Longer Walk

Go downhill and just after passing a barn on the right, take the footpath on the left, diagonally across the field and later passing a residence on the left before meeting the road. Turn left and follow the road to the right, ignoring a private drive which goes straight ahead. After 600 metres, turn left onto a footpath. Cross the private drive and pass a wood on the left and return to the road by the church. Here turn right and rejoin the main walk, Point B.

Point B - Shorter Walk – Main Walk

At the church, turn left and pass the old school house on the left and a lovely old cottage named 'Centuries' built in 1673 and village hall both on the right. After the village hall on the right, take the footpath on the left behind the cottages. Follow the footpath with hedge on your right to emerge between a gap in the hedge and enter the next field and follow the track towards trees in the distance. At the trees, there is a large concrete hardstanding with a driveway on the left. Ignore the driveway to the left and continue ahead with a fence and then a hedge and ditch on the left. At the next field corner, go through a gap in the hedge through a thicket to the road. Turn left onto the road and after approximately 125 metres, turn left up the driveway to Harps Farm.

Follow the driveway, keeping the farm buildings on the right and cross a stile. Follow the well made track and cross a track junction until a sharp left turn and a field ahead is reached, overlooking the motorway, Point C.

Point C

Turn left following the track with the hedge on the right, later with hedge on the left and continue following the edge of the field. Cross the motorway bridge.

Turn left and after 200 metres, branch right on a good grit track down to a stream. Cross the stream and bear right on a path leading into a small wood. Continue up the left side of a field to come out by posts into Beldams Lane, (Footpath 72). Walk down Beldams Lane to meet Hallingbury Road. Turn right and after 600 metres, turn left over the railway bridge. Shortly after, pick up the footpath on the right and follow the river back to the Start.

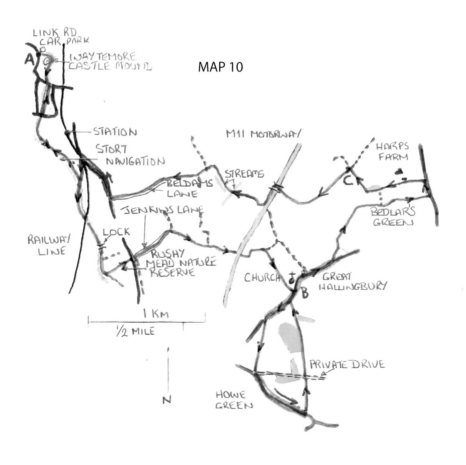

MAP 10

## 11 CLAVERING, LANGLEY AND MEESDEN PARISHES

**Distance: 13.0 kms/8.1 miles**

*This Walk starts from Clavering Village Hall (grid ref TL476320) and crosses farmland in Essex and Hertfordshire. Part of the Walk is close to the infant River Stort and this is an aid to navigation. Refreshment facilities are available in Clavering and the Clavering Lakes fishing area. A point of interest in Clavering is the site of the castle of which very little remains. There is an information board about the castle in the churchyard.*
***Route finding may be difficult on this Walk due to a lack of finger posts and signs.***

Point A – Clavering Village Hall

Exit the Village Hall car park and turn right onto the road passing the cricket field and later 'The Fox and Hounds' P.H on the left. Shortly after, go right at the junction (signposted to Langley). Just before the ford and immediately after the Meadowlands driveway, turn right onto a footpath. Cross two stiles and emerge into open farmland. Follow the footpath over the brow of the hill and down to the hedgerow and footbridge at the bottom. Turn left. Follow the hedgerow to a road. Turn left and follow the road for 450 metres to a sharp left bend. Leave the road and turn right, signposted 'Clavering Lakes', following the driveway to Clavering Farm. At the pond in front, go straight ahead, clockwise round the pond, shortly crossing two stiles to join the footpath. Here, go left and follow the path through the thicket to the end where the path diverges. Take the left path with a hedgerow on left and continue to a byway, Beard's Lane, formerly a Roman road. Turn left onto the byway and after 25 metres, turn right onto the Harcamlow Way.

Follow the path to the end of the field. Bear left and follow the path with ditch and rough vegetation on right. Cross the wooden footbridge through the hedgerow. Cross the track and follow the cross-field path towards a gap in the hedgerow at the other side of the field with terraced housing with three chimneys in the sightline beyond. Cross the footbridge through the gap and follow the footpath to the road ahead, Point B.

Point B – Upper Green, Langley

Cross the road and follow the driveway ahead. As the driveway bends to the right, proceed down a track, later a field edge path which goes through a gap in the hedge and back again near the bottom of the field. Follow the right field edge round to the left and at the second wide gap in the hedgerow, turn right and with hedgerow on the left, follow the path to the road.

Cross the road and follow the footpath to a wide metal gate and stile. Cross the stile into a pasture. Go diagonally left across the pasture to a footbridge. Cross the footbridge and turn left with hedgerow on left and follow this line to a road at Meesden Bury, Point C.

Point C – Meesden Bury

Turn left onto the road and walk 500 metres to Meesden Bridge, identified by white railings. Immediately after the bridge, turn right into thicket and later follow the right edge of pastures going through wooden gates and later a stile, keeping the infant River Stort on the right. After the last pasture and straight ahead, go through a thicket and emerge into a large field. Turn right and follow the field edge, keeping the hedgerow and river on the right. As the river and the field edge turn sharply right, follow the path across two fields marked by yellow topped posts to a farm track. Cross the track and continue on the same line through a series of meadows, meeting up with the river on the right, to a stile at the end of the meadows.

Cross the stile and go along right edge of the field and through a gap into a copse. Follow the path through a wide wooden gate and turn left at the pond ahead and onto a driveway leading to a road. This is Deer's Green.

Turn left and follow the road, ignoring a right turn and after a further 300 metres, turn right through a gap in the hedge onto a footpath, crossing a footbridge and entering the churchyard ahead through a kissing gate.

Turn immediately left, following the left edge of the churchyard.

NOTE: *Observe the information board which provides information about the castle site.*

Exit the churchyard onto a track, leading to a road and proceed ahead to the crossroads in Clavering.

NOTE: *Observe the information board about Clavering village.*

Turn left and return to the Village Hall car park, Point A.

MAP 11

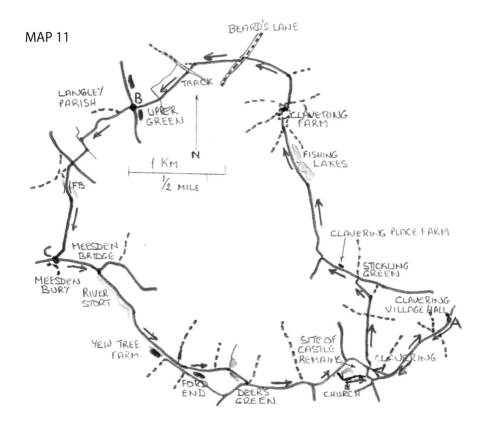

# 12 LITTLE CANFIELD, GREAT CANFIELD, HIGH RODING, PHARISEE GREEN

**Distance: 12.5 km/7.8 miles**

*Park at Lt. Canfield Church (grid ref TL586209). The walk starts from All Saints' Church and crosses farmland and open countryside, passing the church at Great Canfield, followed by High Roding, later passing through the grounds of Pharisee House. The last part of the walk goes along the Flitch Way, part of the old disused railway line between Bishop's Stortford and Braintree. The 'Black Lion' P.H in High Roding is close to the walk and serves meals and refreshments.*

**Route finding can be difficult on this walk.**

Point A – All Saints' Church – Little Canfield
With the church on the left, walk a short distance and turn left, then right along the path through farmland. Proceed past Copt Hall and emerge at a lane. Turn left. After approx. 100 metres, take the path on the right and head across the field to a hedgerow. Turn right and walk with the hedgerow on the left, later crossing a footbridge and going through a thicket. After leaving thicket, turn left and keeping the hedge on your left, walk for about 1 km until you meet a road to the right of a dressage arena. Turn left. Follow the road for 500 metres to Great Canfield Church, Point B.

Point B – Great Canfield Church
Pass the Church on your left. Follow the track round to the right and immediately before the farm complex, turn right keeping the farm track on the left and then turn left and cross the farm hardstanding. Go between the last two barns on the right. After the barns, turn left then right onto a farm track. Turn immediately left, following the left edge of the field with the hedgerow on the left to the corner of the field. Go through the gap in the hedgerow into the next field. Go half right across the field to the corner of a line of bushes. NOTE: *If the path across the field has not been maintained, follow the outside edge of the field.*

At the corner, follow the left field edge to the footbridge ahead. Cross the footbridge over the stream. Follow the path ahead along the right field edge, ignoring the first footbridge on the right. At the second footbridge a short distance further, cross the hedge and turn left with the hedge on the left. Follow the left edge of the field to the corner. Go through the gap in the hedgerow into the next field. Turn right and follow the right edge of the field to the corner. Cross the plank bridge and turn left, following the left edge of the field towards High Roding ahead. Enter the village car park and emerge at the Street, High Roding, Point C.

Point C – High Roding, The Street
NOTE: *To reach the Black Lion P.H, turn right at The Street and it is a short distance on your right.*

Turn left onto the Street. Follow the road through the village for 175 metres to the Old School House on the left. Turn right into the Nursery entrance opposite and follow the driveway round to the left, staying to the left. Follow the edge of the bushes on the left around the perimeter of a small pasture to a footbridge on the left. Cross the footbridge into the field. Turn left and cross the field heading to the right of an electricity pole. Continue to the byway beyond. Turn left. Follow the byway to the road. Turn right onto the road, continuing for 225 metres, passing a cricket ground on the left. Turn left onto a path after Magdalen Cottage.

Follow the path for 1 km until the path changes into a lane. Follow the lane for 80 metres and then turn left onto a grassy track after passing cottages.
Follow the track to a lane. Turn left. Follow the lane to the main road. Cross the road, turn left and immediately right, following the path towards Brands Farm. At the hedgerow ahead, turn right and then bear left into Brands Farm and then immediately right, exiting the farm which is on the left. Cross a pasture to the hedgerow ahead.
Go through a gap and turn left. Follow the left edge of the field and a line of trees on the left, later through a kissing gate and onto a pebble track.
NOTE: *Observe the landscaped gardens of Pharisee House on the left.*

Continue ahead and emerge at an ornate iron gate which leads onto a road. Point D.
Point D – Pharisee Green
Turn left onto the road. Follow it to a T Junction and turn right.
After 100 metres, turn left onto a byway. Follow this byway to the A120 dual carriageway. Continue on the path, (signed for the Flitch Way), keeping the carriageway to your right.
NOTE: *Here the byway converts to a bridleway and cycle network path.*
Follow the path to High Cross Lane. Turn right and after 100 metres turn left onto the Flitch Way. Follow the Flitch Way for 1 km until a road crosses. Turn left. Follow the road for 250 metres to High Cross Villas. Turn right onto a footpath and return to the Start Point at Little Canfield Church.

MAP 12

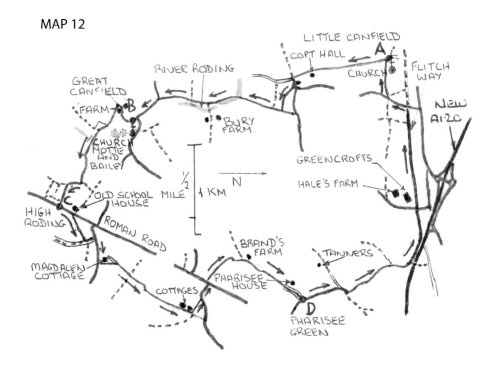

# 13 MUCH HADHAM, STANDON LODGE FARM, LITTLE BALSAMS

**Distance: 9.0 kms/5.6 miles**

*Park on the High Street in Much Hadham near Ye Olde Red Lion Hotel, no longer a hotel, but private residences, distinguished by its eye-catching sign (grid ref TL 428197). This is a walk mainly across farmland with fine views of the East Hertfordshire countryside.*

Point A – Ye Olde Red Lion, Much Hadham

With Ye Olde Red Lion Hotel on the right, walk along the High Street for 250 metres. Turn right onto a bridleway, Cox Lane, passing Tudor Cottage on the left. Ascend for 400 metres and turn right through a gap and cross a field for 50 metres to a gap in the hedge. Turn left and follow the right edge of the meadow and at the end, cross a plank footbridge and turn right.

Follow the right edge of the field and after 200 metres, turn right through a kissing gate into another field. Walk diagonally left across the field to the corner. Go through another kissing gate into a garden with trees.

NOTE: *This is a Public Right of Way across gardens of a private residence, New Barns. Please keep dogs on leads.*

After a few metres, turn right through a gap in the hedge into another garden. Follow the right outside edge of the garden to a corner and exit the garden. Turn left onto a lane and continue ahead, initially with the hedgerow on the left, later on the right. Pass a wood, 'Vineyard Spring' on the right. At the corner of the wood as the lane sweeps to the left, continue ahead through a gap onto a right field edge.

Follow the grassy verge between two fields.

Continue through Standon Lodge Farm. Exiting the farm, with the lake on the left, emerge at a divergence of tracks, Point B.

Point B – Exit at Standon Lodge Farm

Follow the track to the left, with the lake partially visible through trees. Later, the track goes between two fields bisecting a row of large conifers.

At the corner of a field on the right, as the track bears slightly left, turn sharp right through a gap and follow the right field edge to the far end of the field.

Turn right through a gap in the hedgerow and cross a plank bridge and follow the left edge of a field to the field corner. Turn right and go up a grass verge and pass the beautiful grounds of Little Balsams on the left, later joining the driveway and heading to the road. Cross the road and follow the path for 275 metres to a plank bridge on the left.

NOTE: *On a clear day, the London skyline may be seen slightly to the right.*

Turn left across the plank bridge and pass Bowles Wood on the right. After the wood, cross to the other side of the hedge, with the hedge now on the left and proceed to the road. Turn right onto the road and follow for 125 metres then turn left onto a Restricted Byway. Proceed to Bromley Lane, Point C.

Point C – Bromley Lane.

Turn right and head down the lane. Opposite houses, cross a stile on the left into a field.

NOTE: *There may be livestock in the field. Please keep dogs on leads.*

At the bottom of the field, there are two stiles. Cross the stile on the right and a plank bridge and turn sharp left, going through a wicket gate. Go a further 50 metres and turn sharp right, heading to the right of an electricity pole beyond a fence. Follow the left edge of fields, passing earthworks on the left and later a golf course on the left. Beyond the end of the golf course, follow the bridleway as it bears left, passing to the right of cottages and meeting the road, Point D.

Point D

Turn right and follow the road for 125 metres.

Beyond Lordship Farmhouse, turn left following the bridleway to the bottom of the hill. Cross the River Ash via a well made footbridge. Shortly after, turn right and follow the bridleway to the road, Winding Hill. Cross the road and follow a path with a wooden fence on the right. Enter the woodland, heading uphill and take a right fork heading downhill to a path which crosses in front. Turn right and cross the footbridge over the River Ash. Follow the path past the church on the right and emerge onto the road at a sharp bend. Follow the road ahead to the High Street and turn right to the Start, Point A.

## MAP 13

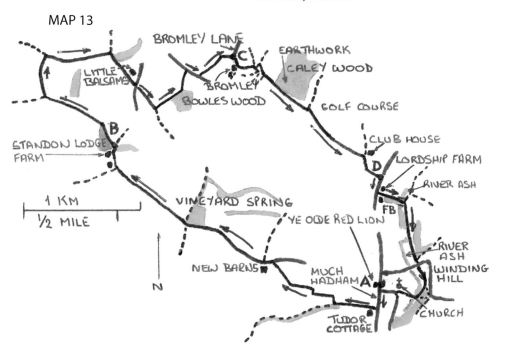

# 14

**BROXTED,TILTY**

**Distance: 6.7 kms/4.2 miles**

*The Walk starts at Broxted Village Hall (grid ref TL573257) in Brown's End Road, Brick End, Broxted, 125 metres from the Prince of Wales P.H.*

Point A – Broxted Village Hall, Brick End

Turn left out of the Village Hall car park and walk a short way and just before the delimit sign, take a footpath to the left. Follow it all the way to Moor End Farm, alongside a field hedge most of the way. At Moor End Farm, follow the road ahead, then bearing sharp left, then sharp right, continuing a short distance to the road junction, Point B.

Point B

Turn right for 75 metres and then left onto an unsigned footpath with hedgerow on right. Keeping in the same direction, continue across a field to reach another road. Turn right along this road, passing The Great Barn, Abbey Barn, Tilty Grange, Pumpkin Hall and Woodlands on the left. At the sign for Tilty Church, turn left to the Church, St. Mary the Virgin, Point C.

Point C – Tilty Church, St Mary the Virgin

NOTE: *This 12th century church was originally a chapel attached to the Cistercian abbey of Tilty.*

Go through the church car park and through a kissing gate and head down the meadow towards a disused watermill at the bottom.

NOTE: *Remains of the abbey can be seen on the right in the meadow.*

Go through the gate, turn right and pass the disused mill on the left, then turn immediately left onto a footpath. Continue along an embankment for 200 metres and cross a concrete bridge and continue with a stream on the left.

NOTE: *The stream may not be immediately visible due to dense vegetation.*

Just before a 5-bar gate, turn left across two streams and then over a stile. Turn right, following the lower edge of three fields, with a small stream on your right. There is a stile between the second and third field. Curve round to join a clinker track which leads to a road. Cross the road and keep ahead along the lower edge of a long meadow, which may be quite muddy, to meet another road with houses, Point D.

Point D – Malting Bridge

Turn right and walk up the hill as far as the turning signposted to Tilty. Here, turn left and immediately right onto a field edge path with hedgerow on the left. Follow the track between two fields, ignoring a path which branches to the right. Continue to the sewage beds on the left. Immediately after the sewage beds, turn right and then left with tall hedgerow on the left, which is the definitive path, until the road is reached. An alternative route is to keep straight on to the road after the sewage beds, passing the Dutch Barn on the left.

CAUTION

This is a fast busy road.

Turn left and follow the road, using the verge as much as possible and continue for 550 metres. Go to the left of the Prince of Wales P.H and take the left fork of the road back into Brown's End Road.

After another 125 metres, arrive at the Start at the Village Hall, Point A.

MAP 14

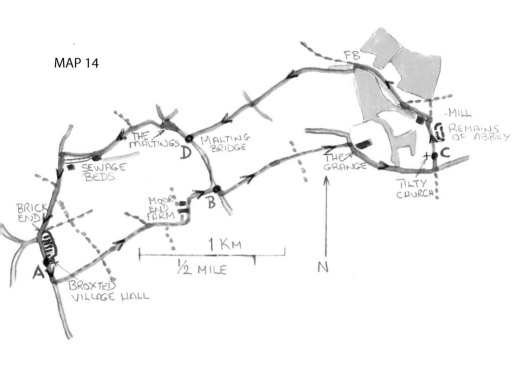

- FB
- THE MALTINGS
- MALTING BRIDGE
- D
- SEWAGE BEDS
- MILL
- REMAINS OF ABBEY
- THE GRANGE
- C
- TILTY CHURCH
- BRICK END
- MOOR END FARM
- B
- A
- BROXTED VILLAGE HALL

1 KM

½ MILE

N

# 15 BRENT PELHAM, MEESDEN, ANSTEY, MEESDEN

**Distance:**

**Main Walk: 12.2 kms/7.6 miles**

**Short Walk: 8.0 kms/5.0 miles**

*Park at the Church of St. Mary the Virgin at Brent Pelham, (grid ref TL433307). There is a small parking area in front of the Church. There is a short Walk and a longer main Walk. Most of the Walk is across farmland and country tracks, with some road walking in the villages.*

Point A – Brent Pelham  Church

With the church entrance on the left, turn left and go downhill, passing 'The Black Horse' P.H on the right. Continue along the road, ignoring the road to Anstey on the left. After a further 250 metres, turn left onto a bridleway. At the other side of the field, cross a stream/ditch and hedgerow via a wide earth bridge. Continue bearing slightly left across the next field to the line of trees. Go through a thicket, later with field on right to the road at Meesden, Point B.

Point B – Meesden

Cross the road and follow the track for 250 metres to a left bend. Here, bear right following the right edge of the wood to the corner. At the corner, bear left, still with the wood on the left. At the next corner of the wood and hedgerow, go through gap, now keeping a hedgerow on the left, field on right.

NOTE: *This section can be very overgrown.*

Continue ahead to a sharp turn on the path. Turn left, then immediately right and head for a wood. This small wood is diamond shaped. Follow the path, keeping the wood to the left, then entering the wood, but keeping close to the outside edge in an anti-clockwise direction.

Emerge from the wood, with ditch and hedgerow on left, field on right.  Go through gap in line of trees ahead.  Turn left onto a grassy track, Roper's Lane, which crosses in front.  Later, the track turns right, then sharp left, then sharp right again.  Here, follow the path for approximately 100 metres and then follow round to the left.  Continue up the gradient for 300 metres to a cross track junction, Point C.

NOTE: *On the right is Scales Wood.  The longer main Walk goes through the southern section of this wood.*

Point C – Shorter Walk

Continue ahead for 75 metres to the road at Lower Green.  Turn left and follow the road back to the junction of the track and the road at Meesden, which was Point B on the outgoing route.  Re-join the main Walk back to Brent Pelham.

Point C – Main Walk

At the cross track junction, turn right and follow track for 300 metres.  Turn right and go to the corner of the wood.  Turn left and follow the path along the edge of the wood on the right, later crossing a track and entering the wood at a wooden footbridge and onto a wide track through the wood.

NOTE: *The edge of the wood to the right of the track marks the Hertfordshire /Cambridgeshire county boundary.*

Emerge from the wood onto the Hertfordshire Way.  Turn left and go between farm buildings and head for the road, Point D.

Point D

At the road, turn right and go through Anstey, passing the small Village Green on the right, 'The Blind Fiddler' P.H on the left and later, the church on the right.

At the church, follow the road to the left.  At the right hand bend at the bottom of

the hill, take a footpath to the left and join a track. Shortly after joining the track, there is a hedgerow on the left.
Walk to the left of the hedgerow, ignoring a footbridge on the left. Cross a ditch with a concrete footbridge. Cross a field, heading for the left edge of the field.
Follow the left edge of this field and at the corner, go through a gap in the hedgerow and into a thicket.
Emerge from the thicket and cross two wooden footbridges close together.
Follow the right edge of a field. At the right corner of the field, go through a gap in the hedge and then follow the left edge of two fields, the last of which is a very large field.

At a track crossing in front, go through a kissing gate, slightly to the left into a small field.
Walk diagonally across this small field to a finger post close to the back of a house. Go along the path to the left of the house and emerge at the road.
Turn right onto the road. Follow the road to the junction of the track and road at Meesden, which was Point B on the outgoing route.

Point B

Turn right at this point and follow the route back to the road near Brent Pelham. Turn right and follow the road through Brent Pelham, passing the 'The Black Horse' P.H on the left and returning to the Start at the church.

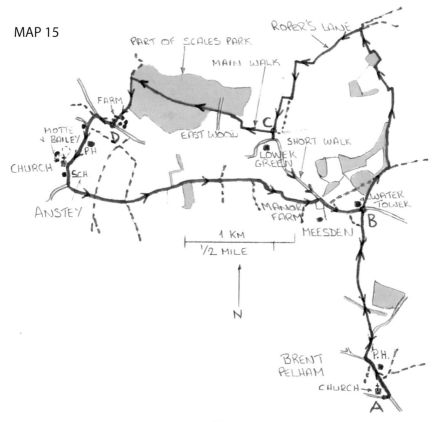

MAP 15

# 16

## HENHAM, HENHAM LODGE, AMBERDEN FARM, RIVER CAM

**Distance: 6.0 km/3.7 miles**

*Park on the lane, in front of St. Mary's Church, Henham, grid ref TL544285. This could be a good winter walk as a lot of it is on firm farm tracks with fine views and also follows the infant River Cam.*

*Although this is an easy walk to follow, the fields are huge so be prepared for long walks between directions.*

Point A – St. Mary's Church, Henham

With the Church on the left and 'The Cock Inn' P.H on the right, walk down the road to a farm track on the right which you meet as the road bears left by a small grass triangle. Walk down the track ignoring the footpaths and tracks to both the left and right and keep straight on to industrial buildings at Henham Lodge. Turn left between these and some newly converted barns on the right and continue to the end of their gardens. Turn right at the bottom of the gardens onto the farm track. Follow this track across farmland, later going under electric power lines, until Amberden Farm is reached. On reaching some barns on the left, go straight ahead keeping Amberden Hall to your right. Continue past the lake to the road ahead.

Point B

Turn left along the road and continue for 425 metres until you reach a footpath on the left. Take this grit track uphill and then go across the cross track into a long meadow. At the far end of the meadow follow the field edge path on your right until you reach the footbridge over the River Cam in the far right corner of the field.

NOTE: *This is the infant River Cam. It is lovely in spring with bluebells, oxslips, cowslips, anemones and many other species.*

Cross the bridge and turn left keeping the river to your left. Continue along the bank for 400 metres until you reach a footpath to the right leading to Priors Wood. Continue a short way past this sign until you reach a bridge over the river, Point C.

Point C

Cross the bridge and then a stile into a meadow. Cross this meadow to the gate in front. Go through the gate into the field by the pylon.

NOTE: *The Definitive Path follows the left side of the hedge. An easier route may be the right hand side of the hedge, which can be reached through a gap in the hedge by the pylon.*

Following the Definitive Path, follow the right field edge to the top of the field and go through the gap in the hedge and continue along the same line, following the path downhill to the Fishing Lake. Keeping the lake on your right, continue along the track as it bends left until it brings you back to the farm track you started on.

Turn right on the track and continue uphill back to your starting point at Henham Church.

FOOTNOTE: *For many years the part of this walk along the banks of the Cam was unusable due to erosion of the footpath. Our late Footpaths Secretary, Gordon Hands, worked tirelessly for over twenty years to persuade Essex County Council to rebuild the banks and restore the path. He eventually succeeded and we include this walk as a tribute to his efforts.*

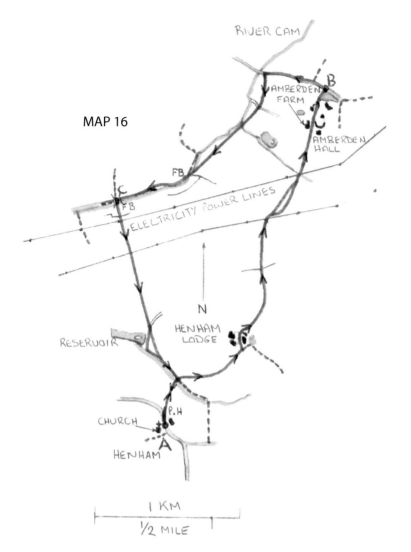

MAP 16

RIVER CAM

AMBERDEN FARM

B

C

AMBERDEN HALL

FB

C

FB

ELECTRICITY POWER LINES

N

HENHAM LODGE

RESERVOIR

P.H

CHURCH

A

HENHAM

1 KM

½ MILE

# 17

## WARESIDE AND LEE VALLEY

**Distance: 12.2 kms/7.6 miles**

*Park at Wareside Village Hall Car Park, (grid ref TL395155) at the back of the Chequers Inn P.H. This anti-clockwise walk has a wide variety of terrain, taking in woodland, farmland, parkland, meadows and open countryside with well made footpaths and bridleways. It has spectacular views of the Lee Valley and crosses the course of the old disused Stanstead Abbotts to Buntingford railway line.*

<u>Point A – Wareside Village Hall</u>

Exit the car park and turn right and immediately right again at Hermitage Cottage. Within a few metres, turn left at Bourne Cottage. Go up a narrow shady path to a road. Turn left onto the road and then right at the School junction. Proceed along the road to a sharp left bend. Leave the road and proceed ahead onto a shingle track, later an earthy track through a tunnel of trees. Continue on this path emerging at Newhole Farm on the left. Turn sharp right onto a wide track, later passing the outskirts of Ware to the right until the road is reached. Cross the road to the entrance of Widburyhill Farm, Point B.

<u>Point B – Widburyhill Farm</u>

Go through the farm and emerge onto a track, later observing the fine views of Lee Valley ahead. Proceed down the track into the valley. At the bottom, by a footpath sign and before the road, turn sharply left and descend into woodland. Cross a well made wooden footbridge over the River Ash and bear right towards a stile. Climb the stile and turn left onto a track (the old railway line) and immediately leave the track and climb the stile on the right into parkland.

Follow the left edge of the parkland until the end, where a track merges from the right. Continue to a T Junction, Point C.

<u>Point C</u>

Turn right and head uphill entering woodland, later with open countryside on the left. Continue to a prominent cross path junction. Turn left and follow the path through open countryside to Little Briggens. Turn right and descend down the gravel track to a forked track junction. Take the left track and follow for 100 metres and turn left and over a wooden footbridge.

Follow the right edge of the field, continuing along this line for a kilometre, passing between two large woods, until the Harcamlow Way merges from the left. Turn right, then immediately left through a gap in the hedge and after 15 metres, go right and head diagonally across a field to the bottom left corner of the field. Here, bear left onto a grassy track to a T Junction. Turn left onto a tarmac track and continue to the entrance of Fillets Farm. Take the right fork and pass the farm on the left to a T Junction, Point D.

<u>Point D</u>

Turn left and follow the track for 500 metres and take the second of two left turns onto a footpath.

Follow the path, through a plantation and then cross a field, aiming for a point slightly to the left of Thistly Wood ahead. Go through a gap in the hedge, crossing a small plank bridge.

After Thistly Wood, cross another field and at the other side of the field, climb the stile and descend a meadow to a metal gate and stile. Climb the stile and cross the track.

NOTE: *The track is the course of the old disused railway line between Stanstead Abbotts to Buntingford.*
Follow the path alongside the River Ash, later crossing the footbridge on the left. Follow the footpath to the road.

*CAUTION*
*Take care at this road as there is no pavement.*
Go left at the road and return to the Village Hall, Point A.

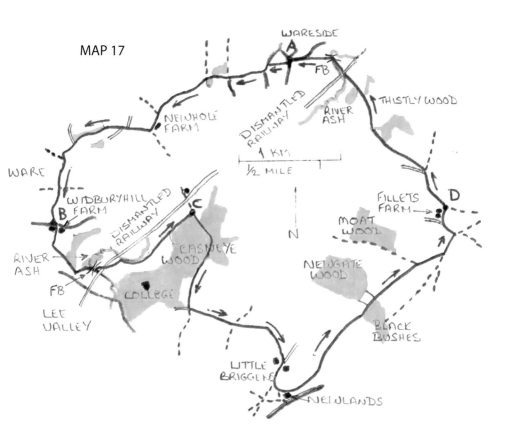

MAP 17

# 18 RICKLING, WICKEN BONHUNT

**Distance: 9.2 kms/5.7 miles**

*Park in front of All Saints' Church at Rickling, (grid ref TL498314). Parking is limited and it is advisable to avoid Sunday mornings when church services may be taking place. This walk is mostly on ancient trackways on high ground offering extensive views over the surrounding countryside. There will be a wealth of early flowers in the spring, skylarks in the summer, nuts and berries on the ancient hedgerows in the autumn and bracing air in the winter.*

Point A – All Saints' Church, Rickling

With Rickling Church on your left, take the road to the left, passing the thatched, rendered and timber-clad barn on the right. After Appletree Cottage on the left and before the large modern barn, turn left onto a signposted bridleway which leads across open fields. After a double bend, the track drops down and veers to the right through the hedge and then follows the field edge for 150 metres where you turn left to go down the slope with Wicken Bonhunt Church visible at the bottom. NOTE: *The double bend is not part of the definitive path, but is the path which is normally used. The definitive path is across the field but is not waymarked and is not used.*

The track emerges onto the B1038 road at Wicken Bonhunt opposite the Coach and Horses P.H, Point B.

Point B – The Coach and Horses P.H

Opposite the Coach and Horses P.H, turn right. After 50 metres, beyond the road running back behind the pub, take the bridleway signposted to the left up another track which soon leads to metal gates.

Carry straight on past the Dutch barn into open countryside once again. At the high point where a footpath comes in from the left, carry straight on down the hill with the view of the M11 running northwards near Audley End Station and with Saffron Walden visible in the distance. Continue to the bottom of the slope, where there is a track junction, Point C.

Point C

Here, take a sharp turn right up the hill towards a small copse of trees at the top. Follow this track which descends under the M11 towards Newport. About 400 metres after the motorway, turn right onto a footpath which starts along a short made up road past an industrial building. This path will lead to meadows. Continue along the path to the ford and cross the footbridge over Wicken Water to meet the B1038 road, Point D.

Point D

Turn right to follow the B1038 road for about 200 metres and take the byway to the left immediately after the motorway bridge.

Only 20 metres along this byway, turn right down a little bank onto a section of the old road. A short way along this road, take the footpath to the left by the double gates. NOTE: *The ancient St. Helen's Chapel is on the right. In its walls, notice the variety of different stones which would have been deposited in the area after the last ice age.* The path bends to the left over a concrete bridge, after which leave the track and head straight on up the field with the hedge on the left. Part way up the field, this path leads left through trees and onto the byway.

Turn right and follow the byway for about 600 metres.

NOTE: *This used to be a well-used route from the Saffron Walden area towards London via Puckeridge. This is a byway and is open to any vehicle.*
Where a track crosses by a large ash tree take the left hand fork. This track soon turns left up a slope by a wood and at the top of the wood, turn right.

Follow this well-used farm track for 900 metres to a junction with a waymark post. Follow the track round to the right by the pair of oak trees and this track will lead back to the byway which will come in from the right. Turn left and follow the byway back to Rickling Church.

MAP 18

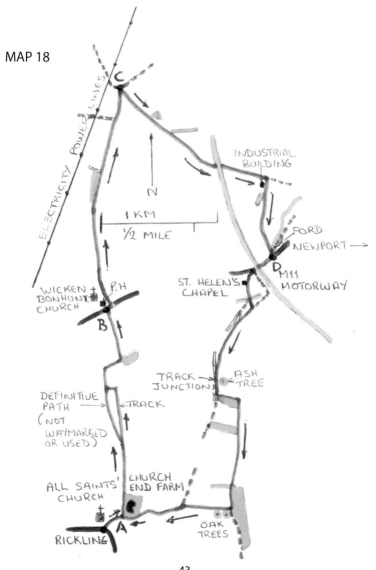

# 19 THE MATCHINGS

**Distance: 10.5 kms/6.6 miles**

*The Walk starts at the Chequers P.H, Matching Green at grid ref TL536110. There is space for parking at the Green. The route goes through Matching, Newman's End, Matching Tye and back to the Start at Matching Green. The Walk takes in open countryside and crosses a disused airfield. The last part of the Walk crosses arable farmland. It is recommended that Wellington Boots or other sturdy walking boots are worn. If field crossings have not been maintained and conditions are muddy, there is the option of walking field edges. There are refreshments in Matching Tye and Matching Green.*

Point A – The Chequers P.H

From the Chequers P.H and with the Green on the left, head for the road junction and turn right. Pass the school on the right. Turn left at the road junction. After 250 metres and at a right hand bend, turn left onto a bridleway. After 25 metres, bear left and follow the concrete bridleway, later crossing the disused airfield to a road. At the road, turn left. After 200 metres and at a left hand bend, follow the definitive path across the field to the hedgerow. Turn right onto the bridleway. If the path has not been maintained, there is the option of continuing along the road for a further 200 metres to the hedgerow. Turn right and go along the narrow bridleway to a road, Point B.

Point B

Turn left onto the road. Walk for 200 metres. Turn right onto a bridleway, marked as a byway on older maps. After 500 metres, emerge at Kingstons Farm.

Turn right onto the road. Follow the road to a T Junction. This is Downhall Road. Turn right and shortly turn left after Stonehill Cottage. Follow the road to Matching Church, Point C.

Point C – Matching Church

Go through the Church graveyard. Exit through a kissing gate and bear right diagonally. Turn left over a well made footbridge. Cross the bridge and then cross a short pasture to a stile. Turn right. Follow the field edge with hedgerow on right to a gap in the hedgerow. Cross the stile. Turn left onto a wide pasture. Go along this wide pasture, eventually sweeping to the left. At the waymarked footpath on the left, cross a stile. Go through a thicket to a field edge. Turn right. Follow the field edge to the field corner. Turn left. Follow the field edge with hedgerow on the right to a track junction. Turn right. Follow this bridleway to a driveway. At the driveway, turn left and follow the driveway to the T Junction at Point D, Newman's End.

Point D – Newman's End

Turn left. Follow the road for 300 metres. At the sharp left bend, take a footpath to the right. After 150 metres, follow the footpath to the left, ignoring a footpath to the right. Keep on the footpath, ignoring the track which later bends to the right. At a field corner with Matching Tye ahead, there are two options:

1) Cross the field to a marker post at the residential area. Go along the narrow footpath between houses. Cross a residential road and go a short distance to Harlow Road. Turn left and head for The Fox Inn on the right, Point E.

2) If the footpath crossing the field has not been maintained, turn left and head to the

road. Turn right. Follow the road for 350 metres to The Fox Inn, Point E.

Point E – The Fox Inn, Matching Tye
CAUTION
Take care when walking on the road as there are blind corners.
Pass The Fox Inn on the right. Take the road towards Matching Green. After 400 metres, leave the road at a sharp left bend, turning right onto a footpath adjacent to a stream. Turn right again following the field edge and at the corner, turn left with the wood on the right to a gap in the hedgerow. Go through the gap at the corner of the wood. Turn left leaving the wood behind. Follow the field edge to the road.
Follow the road for a few metres. Turn right.

Follow the field edge with ditch and hedgerow on left.
Follow the field edge round a corner, later reaching a footbridge. Cross the footbridge and head across the field to a corner of a wood. Follow the edge of the wood to the far corner of the wood. Cross the field to a waymarked sign and follow the field edge to another footbridge. Cross the footbridge. Go to the far end of the pasture. Cross a stile and cross another pasture to the road in Matching Green.
CAUTION
Take care at the road. There is a high coniferous hedge on the left which causes a blind spot.
At the road, turn left. At the road junction, turn right and return to the Start at Point A.

MAP 19

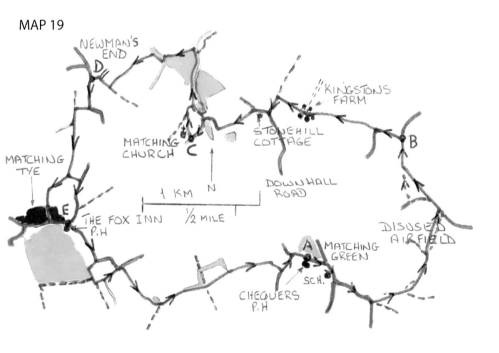

## 20 STANDON, BALSAMS AND RIB VALLEY

**Distance: 8.4 kms/5.2 miles**

*The walk starts at the High Street in front of St. Mary's Church, Standon, grid ref TL396222, where there is limited car parking. This is a pleasant walk which gives fine views. The Walk crosses farmland, using footpaths along field edges and near the end, close to the River Rib, through a watermeadow. Some parts of the Walk, particularly the bridlepaths are muddy in the winter months. There is a bus service 386 to/from Bishop's Stortford. (Thurs and Sat only).*

Point A – St. Mary's Church

Starting from the Church in the High Street, with the church on your left, walk to the junction of Papermill Lane, where there is a small green on the right with a puddingstone and oak tree.

NOTE: *The oak tree was planted in 1911 to commemorate the coronation of King George V.*

Continue along Hadham Road and immediately after the last cottage on your right (a Victorian terrace of three), turn right up a concrete track. Later, pass the entrance to the sewage works on the left and into a small plantation. Emerge at the field edge, Point B.

Point B

Turn left. Follow the field edge path with a deep ditch on the left. At the field corner, ignoring the uphill path on the right, go through the hedge and continue beside the stream on the left. Continue along the field edge to the corner. Here, join the path which crosses from the bridge on your left and turn right up the hill, following field edge.

NOTE: *There is a bench for walkers to rest and admire the view.*

Continue uphill with Little Balsams on the left to a clear break in the hedge – a waymark shows the way up the driveway to the road, Point C.

Point C

Cross the road. Follow the boundary between two fields. Pass a footpath which goes off to the left.

NOTE: *At this point and on a clear day with no cloud, the City of London skyline may be seen ahead and slightly to the right.*

Continue ahead and down towards a small spring. Cross the bridge. The path crosses the ridge that divides the Rib and Ash Valleys. Pass a trig point on the left. Shortly after the trig point and at the field corner, bear left and proceed to a bridlepath which crosses in front.

*Note: Through the gap in the hedge, there is a bench to sit and admire the view.*

Turn right. Keep the hedge, ditch and copse on the left until it crosses another bridleway. Turn left and then right through the line of the hedge. With the hedge and the ditch now on the right, ignore a footpath on the right. Continue to a T Junction, Point D.

Point D

Turn right. Follow the track, passing a wood on the right and a field on the left to a sharp left turn.

NOTE: *The definitive path crosses the field from Point D.*

Turn left and then right and with the hedge on the left, go up the track to a junction on the left.

NOTE: *There is no Public Right of Way straight on.*

Turn sharp left and follow the bridlepath with the hedge on the right to the corner of the field. Turn right with the ditch on the right, later passing a copse and pond on the left. Go downhill until a path to the right towards Arches Hall is reached. NOTE: *Here, there are two oak trees on either side of the bridlepath.* Turn right. Follow the path for Arches Hall which later becomes a concrete path. Pass to the left of the white gates and go between farm buildings and Arches Hall to the left. Turn left at a T junction and exit the farm onto a lane. Go steeply downhill to the minor road junction, Point E.

Point E

Turn right to a ford and footbridge. Do not cross the River Rib.

Ahead, a gate leads into a field with a pig shed on the left and hedge on the right. Follow the bridlepath between the shed and the hedge, going uphill. Continue over the hill down to the bottom at a track crossing. Go ahead through a gate and through the meadow to the far end. Go through the gate.

NOTE: *Standon Ford is to the left and the old papermill is ahead.*

Turn right onto Papermill Lane. Follow the lane to the junction of the High Street and Hadham Road.

Turn left by the puddingstone and return to the church, Point A.

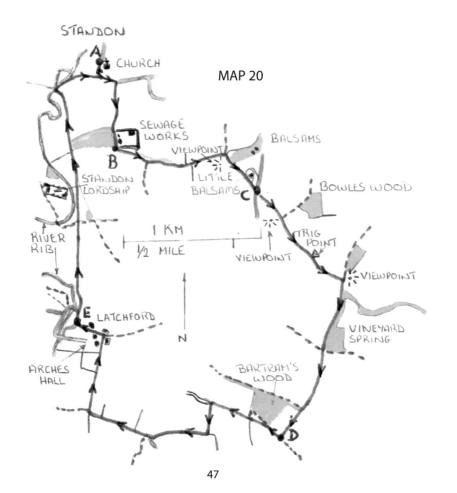

MAP 20

# 21 THE RODINGS

**Distance:**
**Main Walk: 14.5 kms/9.1 miles**
**Short Walk: 10.7 kms/6.6 miles**
*The Walk starts at St. Edmund's Church in Abbess Roding (grid ref TL572114) where there is a small area for car parking. If the long walk is taken, the route takes in the Rodings in an anti-clockwise circular walk, consisting of Abbess Roding, Keeres Green, Roundbush Green/Aythorpe Roding and White Roding. There are refreshments available at White Roding. The Walk finishes by taking the Three Forests Way between White Roding and Abbess Roding.*

Point A –St.Edmund's Church,
Walk downhill from the Church. Turn left on to School Lane. Go to the T Junction. Turn right and immediately left onto a bridleway with hedges on both sides, later with hedge on right. After 420 metres, at a waymarked sign on the right, take the bridleway diagonally left across the field towards the wide wooden bridge, visible beyond a clump of trees.

NOTE: *If the diagonal bridleway across the field is not immediately obvious, carry straight on and then sharp left after a lone oak tree and head towards the bridge.*
Cross the bridge and go straight ahead across the field to the track, Frayes Chase. Cross the track. Head across a field and a meadow to a footbridge. Cross the footbridge over the stream. Turn left and head for the left corner of a field and go through a gap in the thicket. Go through the thicket keeping to the left edge of fields for 750 metres until there is a rough track straight ahead and a bridleway to the right. Take the bridleway to the right and

after 50 metres, there is a footpath to the left, Point B.

Point B - Short Walk
Take the footpath to the left through a thicket. Cross a plank footbridge to a corner of a field. Keep to the right field edge with the ditch/stream on the right. After 150 metres, cross a plank bridge on the right and continue on the other side of the ditch for 575 metres to another bridge on the left. Cross the bridge and head across the field to the main road.
Cross the road and pass to the right of a church. Continue past farm buildings on the left and along a concrete pathway to a cross path.
Take the left path, keeping the ditch/stream on the left. At the corner of the field, climb over the farm gate which cannot be opened, using the stepping plate. Turn right onto the wide grass avenue and turn immediately left and climb over an identical gate. Cross the field, later crossing the River Roding via an elevated footbridge to reach Point D. Rejoin the main walk at Point D on the other side of the River Roding.

Point B – Main Walk
At Point B, Continue for 1 kilometre along the bridleway to the road.
CAUTION
Take care at this junction.
Cross the road and continue through a wood to a road. This is a Byway Open to All Traffic and motorised traffic may be encountered. At the road, bear right.
CAUTION
Take care at this junction.
Walk 275 metres to a waymarked sign on the left. Take the left turn and cross the field. Enter the next field, through a gap in the hedge, keeping to the left edge of the field.

Just before the corner of the field, turn left and into a thicket. Continue to the end and turn right into a cricket field at Cloghams Green. Walk round the right outside edge of the cricket field and along a track in front of a cottage to a track on the right. Turn right and keep on the line ahead.

Follow the left edge of a second field and near a left corner, take a footbridge across a stream and keep to the left edge of a field. At a corner go through a thicket and emerge to the left of Cut Elms cottage. NOTE: *This is the edge of Keeres Green.* (continued overleaf)

MAP 21

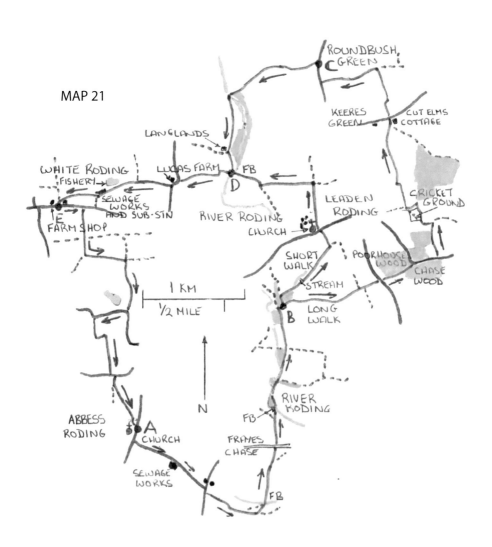

Cross the road and continue ahead on the footpath to a T Junction. Turn left and head for the road. Cross the road. Turn right and follow the pavement to a gravel track on the left, Point C.

Point C – Roundbush Green - Entrance/Exit at Aythorpe Roding Cricket field

Turn left onto the track and later leaving the track onto a path ahead. Later, follow the right edge of the field to a corner of a wood. Take the track with the wood on the left and cross a wide concrete bridge over the River Roding. Turn left and go straight ahead, ignoring the field on the left.

Keep hedge/ditch on left. Cross the footbridge into the next field and follow the path ahead. At the far left corner of the field, continue ahead with gardens and fencing on the right and emerge into the next field with the River Roding on the left to a large raised footbridge, Point D.

Point D – Main Walk - Footbridge at the River Roding

Do not cross the footbridge on the left, but turn right. Follow the left field edge with a ditch/stream on the left for 300 metres and then cross the ditch and follow the right field edge.

NOTE: *The Definitive path continues for 300 metres and then crosses the ditch.*

*If the Definitive path ahead is impassable, cross the ditch on the left via the small footbridge a few metres after the raised footbridge.*

Follow the field edge to the road. Bear left and after a few metres, enter Lucas Farm and immediately turn left following the left field edge. Continue ahead, later crossing two footbridges and passing the entrance to Marks Hall Fishery and the electricity sub-station on the right.

Continue on the footpath. Later, cross a footbridge with stream now on the left to a fence and paddock on the left.

At the far corner of the paddock, turn left onto the Three Forests Way. Continue to the road adjacent to Bretts Farm Shop at White Roding, Point E.

Point E – Bretts Farm Shop, White Roding

Turn left onto the road for 250 metres. Turn right at the waymarked sign. Cross the field path heading towards the third electricity pole to the left of the windmill and then through a gap in the hedge. Turn left, keeping a hedgerow on the left. At the corner of the field, turn right and head to the road. At the road, turn right (Church Lane) and follow for 330 metres to a sharp right bend. Leave the road and turn left into a field and follow the left field edge. Cross the plank bridge. Turn left onto a wide grass path. After 125 metres, turn right at the waymarked sign and cross a field as far as the road.

Turn left onto the road and then immediately right and follow the left field edge to a waymarked sign on the left. Cross a footbridge here. The church at Abbess Roding comes into view. Cross the field diagonally in the direction of a marker post and the church in the distance back to the Start in Abbess Roding, Point A.

# Footpath Problems

Footpath problems can include the following:

1) Obstructions
2) Ploughing
3) Crops and overhanging vegetation
4) Bulls, dogs and other animals
5) Damaged stiles and gates
6) Unauthorised and misleading notices and signs
7) Intimidation
8) Motor vehicles
9) Dangerous excavations
10) Barbed wire and electric fencing

The list is not exhaustive. For more comprehensive information, please refer to The Blue Book, 'Rights of Way - A Guide to Law and Practice' by Riddell and Trevelyan, published by the Open Spaces Society and the Ramblers' Association.

Contacts for Reporting Footpath Problems

Essex:- Rights of Way Team, Essex County Council, County Hall, Market Street, Chelmsford, CM1 1QH

> By post: Essex County Council
> Freepost CL289
> County Hall
> Chelmsford
> CM1 1YY
> Email: prow.web@essexcc.gov.uk
> Helpline: 0845 6037631
> Textphone: 08457 430430

Hertfordshire:- Public Rights of Way Unit, Hertfordshire County Council, County Hall, Pegs Lane, Hertford, SG13 8DQ

> Web: www.hertsdirect.org
> email: row@hertscc.gov.uk
> General Tel: 0300 123 4047

The Rights of Network can be viewed online at:

> www.hertsdirect.org/rowmap

Bishop's Stortford & District Footpaths Association

> Email: contact@walksaroundstortford.org.uk
> Web: www.walksaroundstortford.org.uk

For details of how to join the Association, please refer to the website.

Public Rights of Way
In England and Wales, there are four types of Public Rights of Way (PRoW)
1)  Footpaths: For walkers
2)  Bridleways : For walkers, horse riders and cyclists
3)  Byways Open to All Traffic (BOAT): For walkers, riders, cyclists, horse drawn and motorised vehicles
4)  Restricted byways: For walkers, riders, cyclists, horse drawn vehicles
Walkers may use any of these.  There should be a finger post indicating the direction of the path where it leaves a public road.

Additionally, there are Permissive paths, which are not technically Public Rights of Way.  Permissive paths are paths which the landowner permits the public to use. The Landowner may close a path for one day a year, with the intention that it should not become a Public Right of Way.

-------------------------------------------------------

# The Countryside Code
## *Respect.  Protect.  Enjoy*
### *Respect* other people
- Consider the local community and other people enjoying the outdoors
- Leave gates and property as you find them and follow paths unless wider access is available

### *Protect* the natural environment
- Leave no trace of your visit and take litter home
- Keep dogs under effective control

### *Enjoy* the outdoors
- Plan ahead and be prepared
- Follow advice and local signs

Courtesy of Natural England.  A more comprehensive explanation of the Countryside Code may be found on the Natural England website as follows:
www.naturalengland.org.uk